T0165082

FIGURES IN CHINA'S SPACE INDUSTRY

Who is Qian Xuesen?

www.royalcollins.com

FIGURES IN CHINA'S SPACE INDUSTRY

Who is Qian Xuesen?

By Ye Qiang and Dong Pingping

RC

Books Beyond Boundaries

ROYAL COLLINS

Qian Xuesen (Hsue-Shen Tsien)was a world-famous scientist and one of the founders of dynamics studies in modern China. In China, he has been known by many names such as "the Father of China's Aerospace Industry," "the Father of China's Missile Program," "the Father of Auto-control Science," and "the King of Rocketry."

Qian made a lot of innovative contributions to the fields of aerodynamics, aeronautical engineering, jet propulsion, engineering cybernetics, physical mechanics, and more. Also, he was among the leaders of both theoretical and applied systems engineering in China. Thanks to him, China has successfully built its own rockets, missiles, and space industry.

As a child, little Qian was clever, quick to understand, and he had a very strong memory. His parents were greatly devoted to his education and made sure that he formed good learning habits. At the same time, they didn't forget the importance of his extra-curricular activities, which taught him a love of life and nature. Once when he was little, his father took him to Xiangshan Park (in Beijing) in autumn when the hills were carpeted with gorgeous red-leaf maples. Little Qian pointed to a hawk hovering overhead excitedly and said to his father, "I wish I were him, then I could also fly into the sky." This childhood dream about flying was probably what led him into the field of aerospace engineering when he grew up.

Before the founding of the PRC (People's Republic of China), there were many wars going on in China and it was attacked and bullied by other countries. Seeing this, all Qian wanted was to save his motherland from disgrace and being shattered. He decided that he would go to America and learn the advanced scientific technology. Then he would be able to apply what he learned in his country one day. In 1935, Qian left China to study aeronautical engineering at MIT (Massachusetts Institute of Technology). He was so outstanding in his schoolwork that he finished his master's degree within only one year.

However, after graduating, he changed his focus to theoretical aeronautical engineering (applied mechanics) because the American aeronautical factories, where he was required to practice his learning for his first major, were not treating him with respect because he was Chinese. In October 1936, Qian moved to Caltech (California Institute of Technology) to study under one of the most influential aerospace engineers of the day, Theodore von Kármán. Von Kármán was a professor of aerodynamics and well known in supersonic airflow research, and his teaching was extremely essential to Qian's later extraordinary accomplishments in the field of aeronautics.

California Institute

During his studies in America from July 1938 to August 1955, Qian achieved significant success in many academic fields, including aerodynamics, physical mechanics, rocketry, and missile programs. With von Kármán as his instructor, Qian completed a supersonic aerodynamic research topic and invented the famous "von Karman-Tsien Formula," and became a shining new star in science when he was only 28. His achievement within these twenty years (1935–1955) in America was truly remarkable.

But Qian was often sad, because his success brought no comfort to him when he thought about his home and motherland. In the letters he wrote to his father, he cried over and over again, "I am but a traveler in a foreign land. When shall my wandering life stop?"

In May 1949, as New China was about to be established, Qian's wish to return home became stronger than ever, so strong that he was determined to give up everything he was offered in America—a glittering career and a comfortable life. His determination alarmed the US government, and it issued a warrant to arrest Qian as a communist. Qian and his family were then forced to remain in America for five years.

However, the resolution of Qian and his wife Jiang Ying to go back to China grew stronger over the five years, and they kept asking for permission from the USCIS (United States Citizenship and Immigration Services) to return home. Qian even wrote to seek help from Chen Shutong, who was a Vice-Chair of the Standing Committee of the National People's Congress as well as the best friend of his father. In the end, through the combined efforts of Qian and the Chinese government, Qian and his family were finally able to embrace the motherland they'd been yearning for such a long time.

发愤图强

One month after his return, Qian was visiting the People's Liberation Army (PLA) Military Institute of Engineering in Harbin, accompanied by Chen Geng, who was then Vice Chief-of-staff in the PLA. During their visit, Chen asked, "Mr. Qian, do you think we Chinese people can build our own missiles?"

Qian instantly replied, "Of course, why can't we? If foreigners can build it, so can we! We are no weaker or dumber than anybody!" Soon, Qian was appointed as the first President of the Fifth Academy of the Ministry of National Defense, which was China's first institute of rocket and missile science. There, Qian directed the important experiment of the "combined missile"– having a short-range missile carry an atomic bomb.

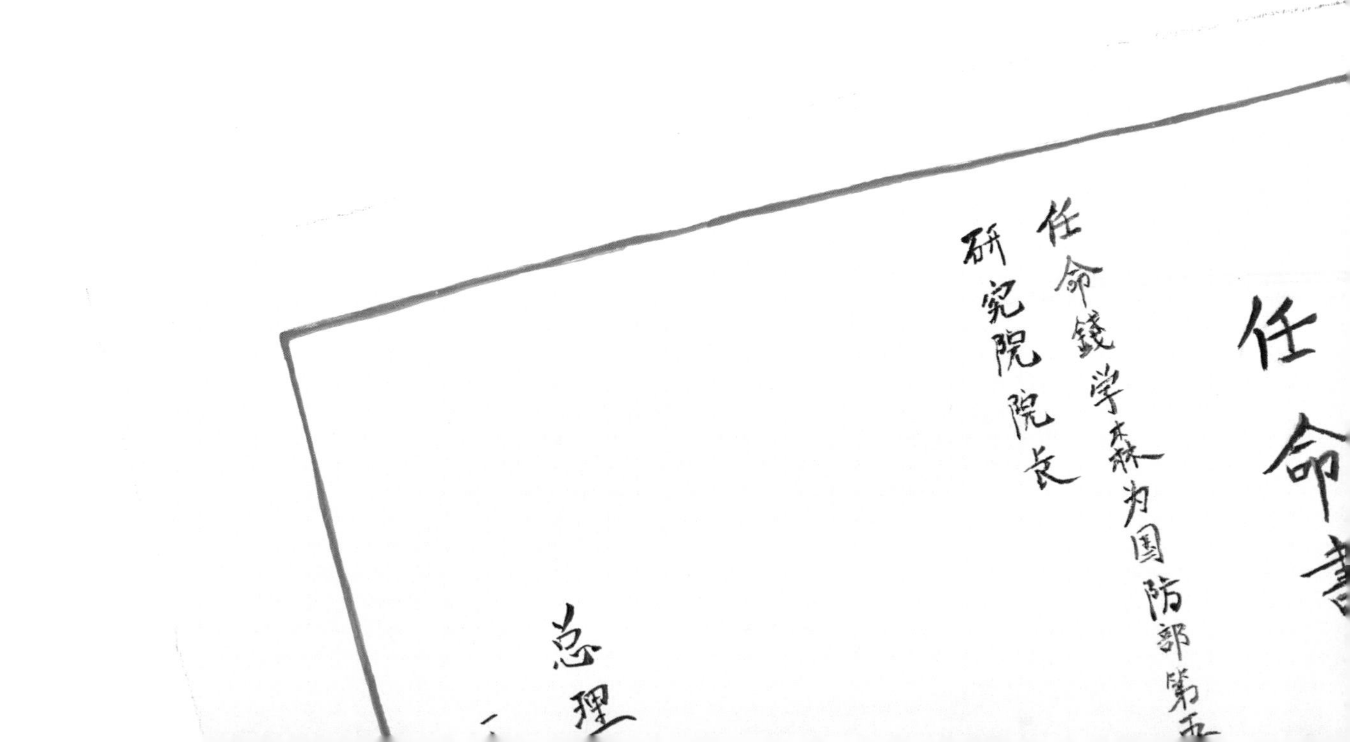
任命书

任命钱学森为国防部第五
研究院院长

总理

It was not easy for China back then to build her own missiles. The country was poor and lacked resources, and its earlier alliance with the USSR was broken. In August 1960, the Soviet Union took back all of its researchers and support and refused to offer any more help in China's rocket science development. But Qian never lost faith in his country and its people. With enormous passion and strength, he fully devoted himself to every part of China's first missile project. Every time when the team was to tackle a major technical issue, Qian would encourage his teammates by saying, "If we did it, you should all feel proud of yourself because you were the reason for our success. If we fail, don't blame yourself. I'll take full responsibility."

"Target hit!" With a loud sound and bright flames bursting from the bottom of the rocket, at 09:02:28 am, November 5, 1960, the testing of China's first missile, the Dongfeng 1, succeeded. In just slightly over two years, China had her own missiles under Qian's leadership.

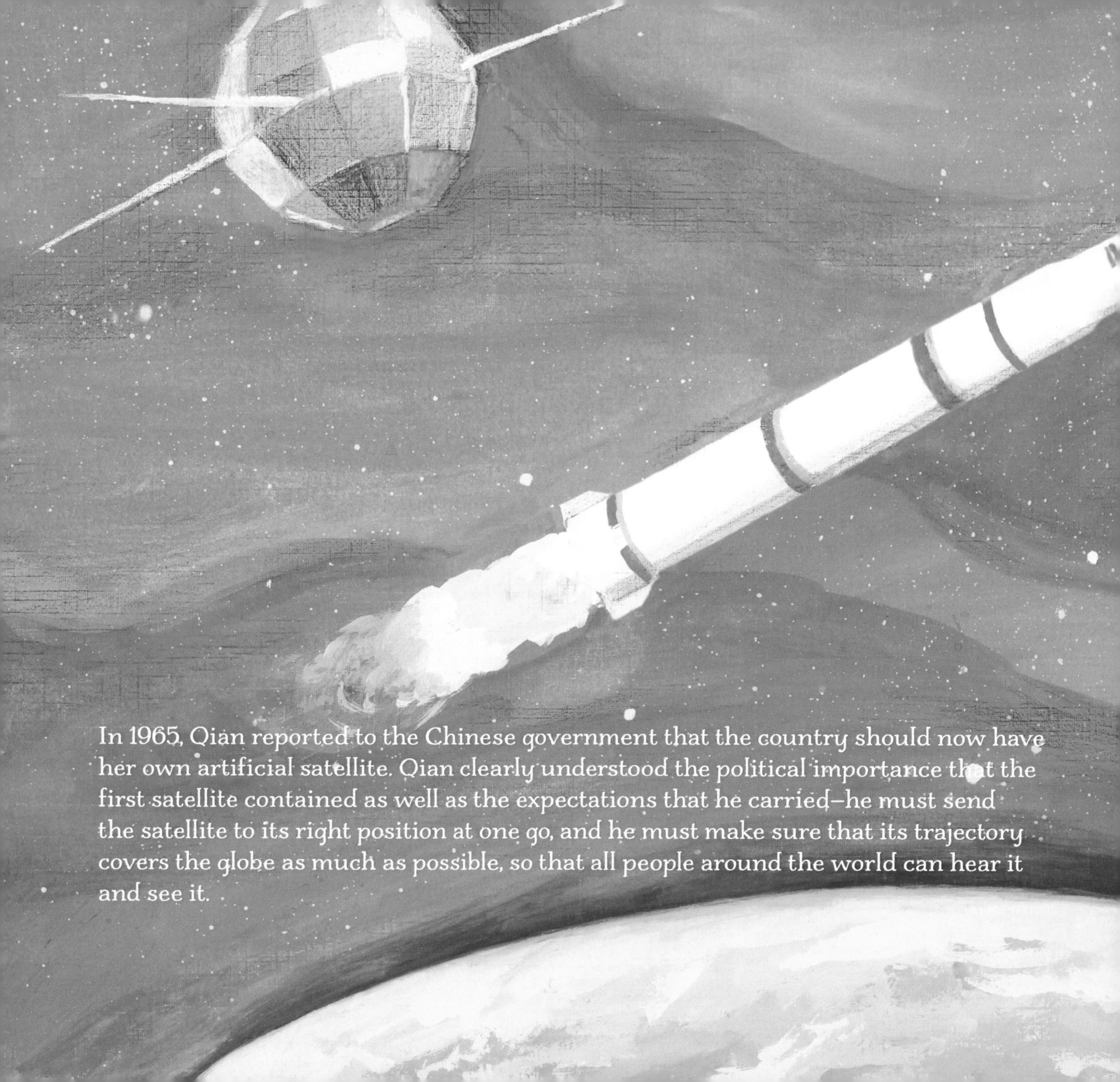

In 1965, Qian reported to the Chinese government that the country should now have her own artificial satellite. Qian clearly understood the political importance that the first satellite contained as well as the expectations that he carried—he must send the satellite to its right position at one go, and he must make sure that its trajectory covers the globe as much as possible, so that all people around the world can hear it and see it.

Five years later, at 21:35:00 pm, on April 24, 1970, the rocket Changzheng 1 carried China's first satellite Dongfanghong 1 into space, and the song Dongfanghong (The East is Red) was heard playing in the sky. At this point, Qian could no longer hold his tears back, as he knew that China has now officially become the fifth nation in the world to have independently and successfully developed and launched her own satellite.

At the age of 95, Qian was honored by "Moving China" as the Figure of the Year for 2007.

He placed his country first; he placed his home second. He viewed science as everything; he viewed fame as nothing. It took him five "long" years to return home, while it took him ten "short" years to build the two missiles for his country. He invented aerospace engineering in China. He paved the path, and he led the way. He was the pioneer, the mine of intelligence, the banner of science, and the example of Chinese scholars.

About the Authors

YE QIANG studied oil painting at Sichuan Fine Arts Institute. After graduating in 2001, he continued to teach in the Institute until 2008. Since then, he's been teaching as an Associate Professor in the Department of New Media Art and Design at Beihang University (Beijing University of Aeronautics and Astronautics). Ye's paintings have been displayed in hundreds of national and international exhibitions, and he has held solo exhibitions in galleries, including the Shanghai Art Museum, six times. Ye's paintings and scholarship can be found in more than 20 academic journals and monographs, such as *Art Observation*, *Art China*, *History to Chinese Oil Painting*, and more. He has also published seven textbooks, including *Basic Techniques in Drawing*, *Basic Techniques in Coloring*, and *A Brief Introduction in Abstract Painting Languages*.

DONG PINGPING is Vice-Secretary of the Party Committee and a member of the Supervisory Commission of the Department of New Media Art and Design at Beihang University.

Figures in China's Space Industry:
Who is Qian Xuesen?

Written by Ye Qiang and Dong Pingping

First published in 2022 by Royal Collins Publishing Group Inc.
Groupe Publication Royal Collins Inc.
BKM Royalcollins Publishers Private Limited

Headquarters: 550-555 boul. René-Lévesque O Montréal (Québec) H2Z1B1 Canada
India office: 805 Hemkunt House, 8th Floor, Rajendra Place, New Delhi 110 008

ISBN: 978-1-4878-0891-4

To find out more about our publications, please visit www.royalcollins.com.